THIS BOOK BELONGS TO:

As salam alaikum, dear friends! I'm the month of Ramadan. I am the ninth month of the Islamic calendar also know as the Hijri calendar.

The Hijri (lunar) calendar is based on the movement of the moon around the Earth. It unfolds in 12 months just like the solar calendar we use daily, yet is about 10 to 12 days less.

Its months have different names than the ones we're used to, starting with Muharram as the first and ending with Dhu al-Hijjah as the twelfth.

The Hijri calendar, being 10 to 12 days shorter, has months that shift through seasons, unlike the solar calendar's months which remain in the same season yearly.

# The months of the Islamic (Hijri) calendar are:

1. Maharram
2. Safar
3. Rabi' al-Awwal
4. Rabi' al-Thani
5. Jumada al-Awwal
6. Jumada al-Thani
7. Rajab
8. Sha'ban
9. **RAMADAN**
10. Shawwal
11. Dhu al-Qi'dah
12. Dhu al-Hijja

And among these beautiful months, I, **Ramadan**, shine as a time of reflection, prayer, and community.

I'm the only month that the entire world eagerly anticipates, watching for the moon that announces my beginning.

Let me share with you why I'm so cherished.

I'm a special guest that brings a time of reflection, kindness, and togetherness.

I am filled with blessings and forgiveness.

In me the gates of heaven are opened and the gates of hell are closed, and every single devil is chained.

Allah placed in me a very special night called **Laylat al-Qadr**. Laylat al-Qadr is also called the Night of Decree or the Night of Power.

Laylat al-Qadr is the night in which the Glorious Qur'an was revealed and angels descend to the earth with abundance of blessings and mercy.

It is a night whose value is greater than a thousand months.

Now, here are some activities Muslims engage in throughout my days.

# FASTING (SAWM)

Muslims all over the world fast. They are commanded by Allah to fast in the month Ramadan.

## QUR'AN RECITATION

The Qur'an, revealed during Ramadan, is eagerly read by many who aim to finish it at least once by the month's end.

# INCREASED DHIKR
# (REMEMBRANCE OF ALLAH)

My days and nights are filled with acts of remembering and praising Allah, seeking nothing but His pleasure.

## INCREASED DU'AS

Supplications to Allah are increased in my days and nights. Believers exhaust themselves asking for forgiveness, guidance, and help in various aspects of their lives.

# PRE-DAWN MEAL (SUHOOR)

I invite you to start your day with Suhoor, a pre-dawn meal nourishing your body and spirit for the fasting day ahead.

# BREAKING FAST WITH OTHERS (IFTAR)

Eating Iftar meal with others, especially people who need extra help, is encourage in Ramadan. It's a way to show we care, share, and are all part of a big family.

# TARAWEEH

Taraweeh is an optional night prayer in Ramadan that unites communities. A part of the Qur'an is read each night for a complete Qur'an experience throughout the month.

# GIVING CHARITY

The blessings in my days and nights inspire Muslims around the world to 10X the spirit of generosity, aiming to support those in need through acts of kindness and donations.

# SPIRITUAL RETREAT (I'TIKAF)

In my final ten days, Muslims do I'tikaf, a mosque retreat focused on seeking forgiveness, salvation, and finding **Laylat al-Qadr.**

# DU'A' FOR LAYLAT AL-QADR

اَللّٰهُمَّ إِنَّكَ عَفُوٌّ تُحِبُّ الْعَفْوَ فَاعْفُ عَنِّيْ

Allahumma innaka `afuwwun tuhibbul `afwa fa` fu `annee

O Allah, You are the Ever-Pardoning, You love to pardon so pardon me.

Tirmidhī

Now, let's talk about my superpowers!

Yes, I have those too!

# SUPER SHARING POWER

I inspire everyone to share their food, time, and big smiles. It's a special part of me that spreads joy and makes everyone feel extra happy!

## SUPER KINDNESS POWER

Everyday, I inspire you to be kind. Maybe you'll help out at home, or just share a smile with someone at school. It's all about making the world a brighter place.

# SUPER SORRY POWER

Super Sorry Power is a special strength that helps you say "I'm sorry" and mean it, fixing little mistakes and making friendships shine bright again.

## SUPER PATIENCE POWER

Holding off on eating until sunset can be hard, but it teaches patience, gratitude, empathy, and strengthens our character, helping us grow kinder and more understanding.

# SUPER CLEAN HEART POWER

Every day, I help you wash away any grumpy or sad thoughts, and fill your heart with so much love that you feel as light and joyful as a balloon soaring up into the sky!

# SUPER HEALTHY BODY POWER

By fasting, your body takes a rest from constant eating, which helps cleanse your system. This practice boosts your health, making you feel strong and revitalized.

"There has come to you the blessed month of Ramadan, in which God, the Mighty and Sublime, has enjoined you to fast. In it, the gates of heaven are opened and the gates of Hell are closed, and every single devil is chained. In it, God has made a night whose value is greater than a thousand months, and whoever is deprived of its goodness will indeed have lost"

An-Nasa'i.

So, dear friends, the next time you think of me, Ramadan, remember, I'm more than just a month.

I'm a month filled with blessings, forgiveness, love, patience, and sharing, bringing health, spirituality, and blessings to your life!

Designed & Published in England by

**Tranquility Hub Ltd**

© Tranquility Hub Ltd 2024

Website: www.tranquilityhub.com

All rights reserved.

ISBN 978-1-914286-14-8 Paperback

www.ingramcontent.com/pod-product-compliance
Lightning Source LLC
Chambersburg PA
CBHW042125040426
42450CB00002B/70